Swing Trading:

An Innovative Guide to Trading with Lower Risk

Introduction

The following chapters will discuss different trading setups that apply to swing traders and day traders. As an aspiring or seasoned trader, you may have boxed yourself only to a limited number of trades. Sadly, this may limit your income and hold your potential back.

You should think about increasing your options and you can do this by reading the different trade setups discussed in this book. Did you know that you could do money trading against the trend? How about trading an industry momentum setup? Or just trading any other type of setup? It is good to consider the options available to you, so that you may have more trading options and also increase your knowledge.

There are plenty of books on this subject on the market, thanks again for choosing this one! Every effort was made to ensure it is full of useful information, please enjoy!

Chapter 1: Breakout Setups: Profit from Range Expansion

Breakout trading can be described as an attempt by a trader to enter the market once the price of a share moves outside a defined price range. Traders often try to take positions in the market that are within a trend's early stages.

A breakout can be defined as a stock price that extends outside predefined support and resistance levels at high volumes. In such situation, a day trader enters the market on a short position if the stock falls below support level or, enters a long position if the stock price rises above the resistance.

This kind of strategy often serves as the starting point of expansions in volatility and major price moves. If a trader is able to properly manage this strategy, the risks are often very limited yet profits will be maximized.

Two Types of Breakouts

Before reading further, you need to understand that there are two types of breakouts. These are:

- Swing high and swing low breakouts
- Support and resistance breakouts

As a day trader, if you are looking to enter a market after the price has moved beyond a predefined range, then you will be breaking out. Any breakout that occurs has to be accompanied by volume.

Also, a true breakout is always accompanied by a bold, huge, candle chart formation that closes out way above the support resistance level. Therefore, as a rule of thumb, the bigger the breakout candle, the better the breakout.

Volatility

The main reason why stock breakouts are crucial trading strategies is that they are the starting points for major price swings and volatility increases. Breakouts are, in many instances, the start of major price trends; they can occur in just about any market environment. However, the most explosive price movements often occur due to price pattern and channel breakouts.

High and Low Breakout Swings

A swing breakout in support and resistance situations is known to happen at times and now, the same rules apply in the high and low swings situation. However, in high and low swing situation, a filter will have to be applied because not all swing highs and swing lows are the same. Our interest in this instance is identifying only those setups capable of offering the best possible outcomes.

As a day trader, you want to attempt breakout trading with the swing lows and swing highs that form a V shape. Such a shape can result when there is a strong rally that is speedily followed by a strong sell-off. This same situation is true in reverse situation. You need to be observant and tread carefully because there are numerous false breakouts that occur in breakout trading strategies.

Distinguishing between Genuine and False Breakouts

As a trader, it is important that you are able to distinguish between genuine breakouts versus false breakout trades. Fortunately, there is a technical indicator that can help determine this -- the Volume Weighted Moving Average, commonly abbreviated as VWMA. It is a basic technical indicator often used in the trade volume analysis.

Surprisingly, this indicator is not as widely used as it should and only professional traders use it adequately. The VWMA is similar to a moving average though it is considered special because it is not just a moving average based on price but more on volume. This indicator is easily noticeable on many trading platforms.

Top Breakout Trading Strategies for Buy Trade

1. Identify a distinct price range and mark it on a chart

You need to identify a price level that can ultimately become your breakout trading level. This is, ideally, the most crucial aspect of breakout trading so you really need to recognize distinct and significant levels. You could also identify V shape swing highs on the chart.

2. Look out for a break then close above its resistance level

As soon as you identify the resistance level, all you have to do is simply wait. What you are waiting to see is not just a breakout, but also a breakout candle that will close above the resistance level. This is often a good indicator that the trend is bullish.

3. Find the VWMA then buy at the breakout candle closing price

You then, need to confirm the VWMA value before proceeding. At this stage, it's important to see this technical indicator move upwards and the moving average trend upwards as well.

4. Put the Stop Loss below breakout candle then collect profit below the VWMA

It is recommended to place the Stop Loss just below the breakout candle, otherwise, you could follow a false breakout. If you need to perform a sale trade, then simply follow the same rules in reverse order. A huge advantage of this trading strategy is trading with momentum. You will benefit from instant rewards and also, learn how profitable your particular trade is. Breakout trading does well even with volatility. If you apply the steps indicated here, you would be able to define a trading plan that can offer a manageable risk and impressive returns when properly executed.

Range Trading

The term "range trading" refers to a trading strategy where a day trader has to identify oversold and overbought areas, which are also known as support and resistance areas. The trader then buys a stock at the oversold area to sell at the overbought area.

Range trading works incredibly well in markets that are declining and inclining with no discernible long-term trend. However, this strategy is not as effective in trending markets even though it can be used after accounting for the market's directional bias.

What is range expansion? Range expansion can be defined as a gradual lengthening or expansion of the price bars of a stock with time. Essentially, the high and low range gets wider and this is usually an indication of a continuation pattern.

How to Swing Trade a Range Expansion

It is an established fact that stocks often spend a lot of time within a certain range. However, they do occasionally move out of range into what is known as a momentum burst. Momentum bursts often last between 3 and 5 days before returning back to range. This is a common phenomenon for most stocks.

The momentum burst of 3 to 5 days typically has a magnitude of 8 – 40%. Stocks with a lower price sometimes have the most spectacular price moves ever. Momentum bursts of this nature all begin with a range expansion. If you scan the charts on a daily basis, then you are likely to come across numerous momentum bursts. However, you need to note that not every single momentum is worth buying into.

It is now quite clear that the most important factor is to understand the momentum bursts. All stocks progress with regular momentum bursts that occur mostly during a bullish run. Stocks can gain between 8% and 20% during such bursts, which sometimes may not have a clear driver. This run tends to last only 3 to 5 days. Lower-priced stocks tend to gain even higher percentages.

This is not a new phenomenon and has been observed during bull market runs for over 100 years. Traders have developed breakout setups mostly because they are predictable and offer very attractive risk versus rewards outcomes.

Chapter 2: Pullback Setups - How to Enter an Established Trend with Low Risk and High Reward

As a trader, you know that there are only two ways to enter a trade, regardless of how many entry techniques you learn. You can only enter on a breakout or a pullback. Understanding this fact is crucial especially for day traders.

How do you define a Pullback?
A pullback can be defined as a situation where the price moves against an underlying trend temporarily. When a stock is on an upward trend, then a pullback is a move that is lower than the trend. However, when the trend is downwards, then the pullback trends higher.

In essence, a pullback describes a security's falling back price after rising to a peak. Traders often view these price movements as short-term reversals of the current trend which signals a temporary pause in the ascending momentum.

Pullbacks: By their very own nature, pullbacks always generate a variety of different trading opportunities after a trend moves

9

lower or higher. Profiting through this classic strategy is not as easy as it sounds. For instance, you may invest in a security or sold short into a resistance and these trends can continue so that your losses are considerable. Alternatively, your security or stock could just sit there and waste away even as you miss out on many other opportunities.

There are certain skills you need if you are to earn decent profits with the pullback strategy. For instance, how aggressive should a trader be and at what point should profit be taken? When is it time to pull out? Basically, these and all other important aspects should be considered.

For starters, you require a strong trend on the markets such that other traders timing pullbacks get to line up right behind you. When they do, they will cause your idea to become a really profitable one. Securities that ascend to new heights or falling to new lows are capable of attaining this requirement, especially after the securities push much farther beyond the breakout level.

You will also need persistent vertical action into a trough or peak for regular profits, especially if the volumes are higher than usual -- mainly because this results in fast price movement once you attain position. It is imperative that the stock in question turns a profit quickly after either bottoming or topping out but, with no sizable trade range or consolidation. It is also crucial that this happens otherwise, the intervening range is likely to oppose profitability during the resulting the subsequent rollover or bounce.

A Closer Look at Pullback Setups

Traders often view pullbacks as excellent buying opportunities once a particular stock has gone through a major price movement. For instance, a share may go through an impressive rise after a positive earnings report, only to experience a pullback when traders begin to take profit. The good earnings report largely implies that the shares will continue the upward trend.

Pullbacks often involve a stock's price shifting to a region of technical support before returning to the upward trend. Examples of the technical support include the pivot point and moving average. As a trader, you should be very careful and observe these areas of support because any breakdown resulting from them could indicate a price reversal and not a pullback. Pullbacks are often referred to as consolidations or retracements by some traders.

Pullbacks versus Price Reversals

As a trader, you need to be able to distinguish between a price pullback and a reversal. Reversals and pullbacks both involve the shifting price of a stock from an initial high. The difference is that reversals are longer term while pullbacks are often short term.

Now, most price reversals will involve a share's underlying fundamentals that cause the market to re-evaluate its worth. Take for instance a firm that reports poor earnings. This is likely to cause investors to recalculate the firm's share price. In some markets, a lower demand for cars could lead to reduced demand for oil, steel, and related commodities and this could be expected to continue in the long run. This is a typical price reversal situation.

However, when the fundamentals of a stock are not affected by the price, then this situation is simply referred to as a price pullback which is always temporary. Traders often get a chance to collect profits in such cases after a stock rallies strongly. Take for instance a company that announces a huge increase in profit earnings, causing the shares to jump by 50%. The stock may experience a brief pullback the following day due to day traders locking in their profits. However, the strong earnings report indicates that the stock will continue to rise in the long term.

In short, pullback situations are often viewed as opportunities to buy into stocks after they experience a huge price increase. The pullback should not be confused with a price reversal which is often a long-term, downward trend and the stock fundamentals are affected. It is important to use technical analysis to determine that the pullback will remain well above key support levels to avoid losses.

Best Strategies to Master Pullback Trading

Pullbacks provide traders with all sorts trading opportunities once an active trend ascends or descends. However, profiting from pullback setups is not as easy as it may sound. For instance, if you buy a stock whose price is dipping, or sell a stock at a loss, then the trend could continue such that you end up suffering even further losses. Alternatively, the stock could gather dust waiting for your next step. Fortunately, there are some favorable technical conditions that can enable a pullback to turn positive once you risk in reverse direction.

A Real Life Example

Take Microsoft Corp shares, for instance. They trade using the ticker symbol MSFT. Now MSFT stock builds a range, for 3 months, below 42 then shortly thereafter the stock breaks out in the month of July. The rise gets to 45.70 points then relaxes for seven days before selling off and losing almost 50% of the initial trend. It then comes into a powerful support on the breakout level. By midday, the stock prints a small candlestick chart that indicates a possible reversal, and rises by more than 2 points. This can then be viewed as a typical and real-life pullback situation.

Identify the Best Entry Price

Once the pullback is in motion, you should look out for a cross-verification. Cross-verification refers to a slim price zone where different kinds of resistance or support queue, opting for a fast price reversal and a powerful movement in the general trend of the stock.

Chances of a rollover or bounce will increase when the zone is compressed as tightly as possible and different types of support and resistance lined up as required. By using your technical analysis tools, you will easily align pullback points with a moving average like the 50-day EMA or a major Fibonacci retracement. For instance, a sell-off to a breakthrough via horizontal highs that aligns with the 50-day moving average significantly improves the chances of a profitable pullback trade.

You should enter a pullback, for instance, where the circumstances are less advantageous by considering resistance and support at levels of price activity are not thin lines and, by maneuvering into opposing price levels.

Now consider another firm, Levi, which portrays a 10-month trading range and displaying resistance at 14 points. It then climbs vertically complete with a huge volume breakout as soon as a new, highly respected manager joins the firm. The news about the manager causes a large one-day gain in share price. This then leads to a sudden pullback that finds support at the top of the range, which is now at 65% on the 50-day moving average as well as Fibonacci retracement.

Trade on Short-Term Pullbacks

There are plenty of opportunities provided by short-term pullbacks. Stocks that experienced recent pullbacks on the stock markets against longer-term upward trends provided investors with excellent opportunities to buy the stocks. Take Moody's stock, for instance. It once traded at a high of $103.34 last November. This share then recouped and settled at $92. By observing the long-term trend, this could easily be thought of as a great point to enter the trade.

As a trader, you can jump in at this point, and buy the stock. Some of the prices you can opt should range between $94.40 and $94.60. Remember to include a stop loss at just below $92. Once you buy the stock, you can then sell when the price rises again to between $100.75 and $101. If you are experienced, you can hold on for much longer and hope the price gets to $104.50.

Another popular share, the MGM, attained trend line resistance in December of 2017. It then fell rather sporadically from that level but the price started stabilizing in early January. To enter this trade favorably, go for $21.25 which is closer to the apex of the January position. You can place a cautionary stop loss above $21.80 and at $18.45. This target price is obviously higher than the low price witnessed recently of $17.25. However, the stronger reversal bars of mid-December indicate increasing buying pressure. If the price drops further below $17.25, then the next price target should be about $16.50.

Stop Loss Measures

There are about three reasons why traders lose money when trading pullbacks. It could be due to a miscalculation that results in entering a trade too early. Another reason could be that you enter at the best price but unfortunately, the reverse trends break logical mathematics and work against you. It could also be due to the rollover aborting because your risk management strategy was not successful.

The third scenario is the easiest to manage. All you need to do as a trader is to place a trailing stop immediately behind your position once it adjusts position to favor you. You then need to adjust whenever the profit increases. Basically, the stop that you require is directly related to the entry price you choose. Once you become a more experienced trader, it will be easier to observe that numerous pullbacks often indicate logical entry levels at various points.

For your stops to be more effective, you will need to wait longer. Also, the pullback will have to go deeper but without affecting your technical analysis. This way, you will be able to place your stops only a couple of cents behind an important cross-verification level. With this approach, you are likely to miss excellent reversals at the intermediate levels but, you will also enjoy some of the lowest losses and biggest profits possible.

In conclusion

Pullback positions taken at the optimum price levels often result in fantastic reward-to-risk profiles which resonate well with a huge variety of swing trading strategies. Trade setups like these often occur on the backdrop of the pullback or short-term momentum even though they are aligned with long-term trades.

A lot of these trade setups on the pullback have rewards-to-risk rations better than 2:1. With such ratios, the strategy will remain profitable even when losing over 50% of all trades entered. However, the risk is never far away even when stop-loss measures are adapted. This is quite a rare occurrence and stop-loss measures work over 95% of the time.

Chapter 3: IPO Setups: How to Find Stocks That Can go Up 50% in One Month

Trading successfully in IPOs requires a solid plan and sufficient technical analysis. Technical analysis is essentially a study of prices changes in a stock over a period of time. The price is often a result of supply and demand. IPOs generally present excellent investment opportunities as well as significant risks so if you are to trade or invest in IPO stock, it is important to have the knowledge, skills, and a solid plan.

Now on an IPO's first day on the markets, demand and supply forces are often raw and aggressive. At this initial stage, there are no resistance nor support levels, neither are there daily chart patterns nor short interest. At this stage, it is not possible to use technical analysis except for intra-day which can be very useful. As a trader, your main purpose at this stage is to work out whether the stock is worth investing in for the short or intermediate trade.

IPO Initial Days

Before an IPO comes to the market, there are two absolutely essential things that need to be considered. These are the size of the float which means the number of shares being offered, as well as the valuation range of the firm. These two factors will greatly influence the performance of an IPO in its initial days at the markets.

The float or number of shares is essential because it refers to the supply. Demand will increase if the supply is low and vice versa. How the valuation figures look like will also affect demand. For instance, if an IPO is priced below par, conservatively, or at par with similar companies, then demand could be high. However, demand at the market in the days leading to the offering will determine the stock's price.

How to Trade an IPO in its Initial Days

If you are to trade an IPO, you need to measure its demand first. Once it opens on the markets, then you can measure its popularity and determine how it will fare in the initial stages. A good IPO should experience an almost instant price increase. It is here that the art of trading an IPO stock comes in handy.

The first lesson you need to learn is to never chase a stock no matter how much you love its fundamentals. Instead, only buy it at the right price. This also applies to IPOs. If the price rapidly increases upon hitting the market, then let it be. Instead, be on the lookout for a range so that it can govern your next move. When a range forms, the stock is allowed to withstand the selling from investors who received shares but want to sell immediately. If the stock is able to hold its grounds after this initial sell-off, that is a great sign.

Now that there is a range, you need to identify potential entry points. For this, you will need to do an analysis based on the patterns appearing on short-term charts. Feel free to use patterns ranging from 1 to 5 minutes or even pivot highs. The benefit of entering an IPO trade or any other trade at a defined technical level is that it allows you to position your stop loss at a precise position within the pattern.

It is acceptable to apply this level versus a level strategy across an entire trading session. Should a stock adapt a different range, then consider the top end of the range as an entry point or trigger and pivot points as the stop loss indicators. Always remember, never pursue an IPO based on hype but on fundamentals.

Using Technical Analysis Tools

Day trading and IPO setups all require that you undertake the necessary technical analysis. First, you need to spot the market trend before beginning your analysis. For you to gain from trading an IPO, the volumes need to be at least 500,000 shares. You should identify the IPO stock you wish to invest in and the find the best stop loss point. Generally, this is normally fixed at 1.5 – 2.0% of the purchase price. Pros normally go for 3%.

Does Technical Analysis Apply to IPOs?

The standard charting methods like the moving averages do not apply to IPO trading. This is because of a lack of sufficient price history as well as, a lack of all other indicators which mostly rely on moving averages. This is why so many market experts simply put all their faith in the IPO launch then hope against hope that it will perform as expected.

One of the best indicators of an IPO's performance is oversubscription at close. However, it might be too late to invest once there is an oversubscription and, buying at the markets once they are listed might be too expensive. Even worse, buying after listing only to watch the share price drop shortly thereafter.

Pricing an IPO is never easy. Even the brokerage firms in charge of the pricing could get it wrong. It is not uncommon for some IPOs to trade well above or well below the offer price. The challenge is that both the brokerage firm and the company want to find the best share price and run a campaign. Using a company's fundamentals at this stage might be a little tricky.

Market Activity after IPO Launch

As a trader, you are only left with market activity once the IPO is listed at the stock market. This is sufficient for a trader to make a suitable trading decision. Your decisions as a trader will be based on the CLB or the count back line. This is a resistance line that tracks price volatility and it is often a temporary resistant line. The CLB is calculated in a falling trend by first counting back 2 higher highs then indicating a horizontal line towards the right-hand side.

Once the line has been drawn, then inference can be made. If the price closes below or above the resistance line, then the downward trend has changed. These closes are then used to make a more accurate determination of entry and exit points. It is only about 3 days later than you can start making decisions. For instance, is the price of the stock going up or down? If the price is trending downwards, you can use the CBL or count back line to determine the best entry point. This is always calculated and determined from the lowest low within the trend. Remember that the CBL is a temporary line so the entry points have to be calculated every now and then.

These count back lines used to calculate the entry points during a downward trend are designated CBL1, CBL2, and CBL3 and so on. Should the stock price rise above the latest CBL line, it will mean that the stock trend has changed its direction. As such, the stock price will need to close above the CBL line to create confidence that the upward trend is sustainable.

This kind of analysis usually takes about 3 days to determine so, it means you will be kept away from the trades until the fourth day. The main objective of this 3-day analysis is, to note the direction of the stock movement then enter the trade once the trend starts heading upwards. This technique is ideal to use with IPO stock. The CBL is determined using data at the end of the day. It provides the trigger points for action.

As soon as you enter the IPO trade, you need to establish a stop loss. The CBL is able to help determine where the stop loss can be placed. As soon as the trend is established, other analysis tools can be used. These include moving averages and straight edge trend lines. However, the focus must always be on managing the stock prudently until these additional tools can be applied. It is important to note just how useful CBL lines are at this juncture. Not only do they help determine entry points but also stop loss and exit points as well.

There are IPOs that indicate a very fast buy signal and even alert a trader to keep off the markets. You can use the CBL or count back line entry technique as a sole trading tool until such a time when other commonly used indicators can be used. These other technical indicators that can apply in this instance include straight edge trend lines, moving indicators, MACD and stochastic analysis.

Techniques for Determining Stocks that Will Rise to 50% or Higher

IPO stocks typically have zero history in terms of volume and price. Many have almost no earnings record with which to evaluate the growth prospects. Chances of volatility are really high even as investors try to work out the ideal value of these shares. One thing traders can do is to use data derived from previous IPOs. There are plenty of analysts who provide data on performance of previous IPOs. Making use of IPO analysis data and information from reputable sources as well as the 424(b) documents that are often submitted ahead of a company's IPO. The data contained in this document includes risk factors, earnings data, company's business and much more.

Also, a trader should regularly examine the daily and weekly charts and other analysis once the IPO stock hits the 3-week mark. Great IPOs will break out of their IPO base volume after a period of 3 weeks, providing an indicator of expected trend. You can also use these charts;

- Short-term or Daily charts
- Intermediate – Weekly charts
- Long-term or Monthly charts

When reviewing the charts, you must ensure that the stocks are on an upward trend. Avoid any IPO that is on a downward trend. You will need to develop a process known as the objective criteria. This provides you with a way to accurately observe happenings on the chart regarding the IPO stock. By learning how to evaluate the charts on a step-by-step basis, you will be able to confidently identify stocks with great potential.

1. Price Action: Taking a look at a share's price action might be one of the best ways of determining how the price will move up. As a matter of fact, price action will be the mainstay and key driver of all other indicators. Basically, if there is no price action then there simply will be no other indicators.

With price action, you should then focus on the highs and lows. The price should be making higher highs and higher lows. If it does not make these higher highs and lower lows, its price will not trend upwards. To confirm that the price is indeed trending upwards, you would need to find an initial price movement from lower highs and lower lows to higher highs and higher lows. Anytime you observe a trend where the highs keep getting higher and the lows also getting high, then you can tell that a share will see a huge increase in price in the coming weeks and months.

2. Moving Averages: By this time, you can begin using moving averages to determine the performance of a share at the markets. There are quite a number of moving averages including the simple, weighted, exponential, and so on. The simple moving average can be used to determine an IPO stock's price movement.

Let us take the 40-day moving average for instance. To work out this average, you will have to add up all the closing prices of the previous 40 bars and then divide the total by 40. This will give you the average price for that time period. You will be able to tell if the price is increasing and if the increase is at a great pace or not.

While the simple moving average does not necessarily confirm that a price will trend upwards, it shows that the market desired for the price to remains strong. Also, the price will often be above the moving average as plotted on a chart. This is yet another great indicator that the price is strong, trending upwards, and likely to remain that way for a long period of time. Should the price move below the moving average, then this might indicate the price will not stay strong for a longer period and hence caution should be taken.

3. Envelope Channels: Another important tool that can be used to accurately visualize the price movement of an IPO stock is the envelope channel. These are percentage-based envelopes that are set below and above the moving average. It is the moving average that provides the foundation of the envelope channel. It could a front-weighted, simple, or even exponential moving average.

The bottom and top channel lines are usually charted similar percentages below and above the moving average. This creates parallel bands that follow price action. The moving average envelope channels are commonly used an indicators to follow the price trend. If the channel formed by the envelopes trend upwards, then the stock price is also likely to trend in that direction. However, should the channel change direction, then you will need to tread carefully especially about continuation in a bullish trend.

The Best Online IPO Research Tools

To effectively do your research on the best IPO stocks, you need access to some of the best tools available online. Here is a look at some of the important ones.

Renaissance Capital: This firm is renowned as the top IPO consultant. They track all the top IPOs trading on US markets and provide crucial markers and indicators that can help determine stock performance and price movement. These IPO experts regularly publish free quarterly and annual reports and provide detailed information about US IPO markets. You can also get all types of analysis, information, data, and statistics about any IPO on their online platform.

IPO Boutique: If you want the best information on any IPO, then this is the site to visit. IPO Boutique is a serious firm with an expertly presented platform that contains detailed information on various IPOs. Here you will find tables that list underwriters and appropriate links to Securities Exchange Commission filings. The firm, however, charges for premium information so if you are serious about trading IPOs successfully, then this is a platform that you can use to get information.

Chapter 4: Momentum Setups: Benefit from Most Powerful Market Forces Industry

Momentum trading is among the crucial trading setups in swing trading. Its effects are widespread and widely used effectively by Wall Street traders to earn billions in profits. Many expert traders believe that implementing one of the best momentum trading strategies can lead a trader to earn huge profits in the short, medium, and long term.

Momentum: In trading, the term momentum refers to the movement of a stock on the market. Basically, when a stock is in motion, it tends to remain in motion unless a force from the outside interferes with this motion. In fact, a market that is in motion is likely to remain in motion. This is the reason why momentum is considered to be such a powerful market indicator. Therefore, any stock market instrument that is on an upward trend tends to continue that trend.

Also, any stock market instrument that goes down tends to remain that way. Therefore, trends once set in the markets often remain that way so momentum is a tool that can be used to determine the best buying and best selling prices. This is because instruments such as stocks, which have positive momentum, tend to also have with positive returns while those with negative momentum tend to result in losses. This is why many traders believe momentum is the best indicator for swing trades.

Why does momentum occur? The simple reason is that rising stocks tend to attract investors while falling stocks tend to attract sellers. This is a simple enough explanation even though there are various reasons why momentum happens. The best momentum trading strategy is, however, based on this simple explanation.

The Best Momentum Trading Setup

Smart trading is actually the best approach to creating the best momentum trading strategy. Actually, there is no need to predict or determine when momentum will occur even though we allow the market to point this out using certain indicators.

Some of the tips we will be using including buying to ascend even higher or sell low to go lower. This means trading our stocks or instruments in the direction of the trend while momentum remains on our side. Here is how to proceed.

1. Start by defining the trend: In any upward trend, we ideally search for a series of higher highs followed by another of higher lows. As few as two higher highs and two higher lows are sufficient to define an upward trend. It is a known fact that the trend is always on the trader's side but without momentum, there may be no trend. To determine a solid momentum, you will also need to take a look at actual price action.

2. Search for actual candlesticks that close near to its higher end: It is common for traders to always desire to use more than one confirmation sign when selling or buying stocks. Confirmation using at least two signs increases the chances of a high probability trading setup. The momentum trading strategy should also include price action.

If you have a price chart, you can easily determine the momentum of the stock by observing the length of the candlesticks. What you will be looking for is a large, bold, and bullish candlestick that end or close near the higher end of the candlestick.

3. Wait for momentum indicator to get oversold: Another thing you need to do is to use the Williams %R momentum indicator. It should be used in a smart way to achieve best results. You need to buy in an uptrend after the best momentum indicator reaches oversold conditions that are below -80 and then gone up to the -50 level. At this point, you will have confirmed both the momentum indicator and the price that the trend is as a result of momentum and chances of price trending upwards very high.

4. Place your protective stop loss indicator: You should place your stop loss marker just below the recent high low level. This is the one that was formed just before the buy signal indicated by the best momentum trading strategy. Also, you can track the stop loss indicator below the most recent higher lows. This way, you will be able to lock-in profits just in case there is a sudden market reversal. You also need a marker that indicates points at which you take profit.

5. Bet on points to collect profit: Any trend with momentum can continue to ride the momentum for a long while to come. As a trader, you want to maximize your profits so you will let the trend ride on the momentum for as long as possible. You will want to take profit when the momentum is about to end. Therefore, look for a break in the structure of the trend and any break below the latest higher low. Take your profits from any of these points. You can also take profits as soon as the best momentum indicators break just below the -50 position.

Summary

This momentum trading strategy makes use of the market's tendency to keep rising in a single and predictable direction if the momentum tends upwards or even downwards. In this case, especially with this strategy, timing is extremely important, especially for the momentum indicator strategy. While timing the market can be quite a challenge, it is possible to use a pure price action that will get you a long way.

Important things Momentum Traders Should Focus on

By now, we know that momentum trading is designed to make use of short-term price activity in a security such as stock and shares. While swing traders can hold onto stock for days or even weeks, a momentum day trader endeavors to buy and sell stocks on the very same day.

However, not all stocks provide ideal trading setups so this makes identifying suitable stocks a crucial aspect of momentum trading. Should you opt for the wrong stock, then you could waste your money and time then end up frustrated. Therefore, you should look out for the following criteria in a sure stock.

Stock Volume

The term "stock volume" simply refers to the total number of shares of a particular stock that are traded. Keep in mind that the aim of momentum trading is to get in and get out on the same day. Because of this, you need to make sure that there are sufficient buyers and sellers in the market. This is why volume is so important. Therefore, find stocks with large volumes so that you can get in and out of trades with ease. Also, high volume stocks are very liquid which means it is easy to dispose of them for cash.

Range and Volatility

If you are a momentum trader, then you need to trade in stocks that are volatile and not range-bound. As a trader, you want to take advantage of the prevailing intra-day price action. The aim is really not to hunt or scrap for a few cents here and there but actually make significant moves in the market. It is better to search for stocks that trade within a $5 range rather than those stuck in $0.35 range for the entire day. The latter provides very little trading opportunities.

Time Frame

Short term moves on the stock market are of great interest to momentum traders. Basically, your interest is hardly in how the stock will perform one or two months down the line. The main aim here is how the stock will perform on a given day and that day alone. This is one of the reasons that you should not be unduly concerned about the underlying conditions or fundamentals of a company. A great company can have a relatively dull day at the market while a poorly managed company could perform superbly at the same market. At this juncture, you really are solely interested in the short-term price action of your stock.

Technical Analysis

A very important aspect of momentum trading is market analysis. Most investors care a lot about the fundamentals of a company while traders are only concerned about the performance of the stock. This is why they always say, "Focus on the ticker, not the company." Price action is very important for day traders.

Now each chart reveals crucial information that you need as a trader. For instance, a stock chart reveals the amount of money investors are willing to part with for a particular stock at any given time. Technical analysis involves the reading and understanding trading charts. Basically, any trader who tries to argue a point based on a company's fundamentals is in the wrong business.

Catalysts

As a momentum trader who is interested in day trading, you need to watch out for any catalysts that can cause a stock to break down or break out. The implications of the catalyst are not really important at this stage but the market's reaction. For instance, during the

Ebola scare in America, a lot of indirectly related stocks skyrocketed. Such price movements are generally not rational but they create tremendous trading opportunities.

High Risk, High Reward Trades

Plenty of people like to compare day trading to gambling. Yet if day trading is done wrongly, the two compare really well. The difference between day trading and gambling is the research and analysis done by a trader and the risk vs. rewards analysis.

Businesses operate very much along similar lines. It is estimated that over 80% of all businesses collapse and die in the first 18 months. This does not necessarily mean that starting a business is akin to gambling. While there are many risks to all things we do, it is important to take calculated risks. In momentum trading, we need to avert risks by choosing trades that have favorable risk versus reward ratios. These are trades that are very likely to succeed and earn you a decent profit.

To mitigate risks in trading, we need to find stocks that have a favorable risk vs. reward ration. For instance, if you just choose a stock to trade, your chances of making a profit are 50/50. This is basically gambling and is never a good trading strategy. But if you study technical analysis, analyze chart patterns, and find favorable risk vs. reward setups, you will definitely lower your risks and increase your chances of successful and profitable trading. Generally, you should not risk losing more than $1 for every $3 you hope to make.

Market Strength

You definitely need to watch out for the overall strength of the market as this can assist you to understand momentum in the market but on a larger scale. What you need to do is observe major indices such as the NASDAQ, DOW, and the S&P. for instance, if one of these indicators is up by about 4% then the market is largely considered bullish, or on an upward trend.

Stock Trends

It is absolutely important as a trader that you focus on a particular stock's market trend. You should ensure that you never go against the market trend as this can be disastrous. Therefore, if a stock spent the entire day trending upwards do not fight it as this will enhance your risks.

Trading Setups

You should also ensure that you focus on trade setups. Plenty of traders often forget this. As you enter a position in a stock, you should have a good reason. Basically, have a good reason why you chose to enter a trade at a particular price.

Sector Strength

Basically, different sectors begin running or operating at different times of the day. For instance, non-lethal weapons stocks rose when police brutality made headlines while marijuana stocks also enjoyed a steep rise when new laws were enacted. It is important to understand any sector that you are trading in so that you understand why stocks are performing or behaving in a certain manner.

Chapter 5: Earnings Gap Setups: How to Profit from Post-Earnings-Announcement Drift

An Introduction to PEAD

In the world of finance and accounting, post-earnings-announcement drift (also known as PEAD), refers to the tendency of an instrument's return to drifting towards the direction of the earnings for a couple of weeks, sometimes even months after an earnings announcement.

Normally, firms that provide great earnings reports in quarterly earnings often see their securities tend to drift upwards for a minimum of 60 days after the announcement. In a similar manner, firms that provide bad earnings reports often suffer from abnormal security returns for a period of about 2 months.

As a trader, you can make a lot of profits by buying stocks with high earnings surprises.

Buying stocks shortly after an announcement will ensure you will profit in the short term. You are able to take advantage of earnings announcements even if the stocks have already moved. PEAD or post-earnings-announcement drift is one of the most profitable and simplest strategies out there.

Trading in Hindsight

Basically, information on earnings once announced, does not reflect instantly on the markets. Markets are very inefficient in various ways. It is this inefficiency that enables you to make money. When a company performs better than expected, share prices are likely to go up and when they perform worse than expected, then prices are then expected to go down. The most important point you need to remember is that the upward momentum of stocks can continue even for two months after positive earnings announcements. This provides excellent opportunities for traders to capitalize and earn easy profits.

Simple Strategy of Earning from Post Earning Announcements

There are a handful of ways to earn money from the inefficiency at the stock market. However, the easiest way is to purchase a stock or instrument that has performed better than expected. It is a good idea to let a day go by before buying the stock. While you might miss out on the initial stock market frenzy, you will also avoid any corrections that may come shortly thereafter.

Take the example of Comcast CMCSA -0.72%. Comcast stock rose sharply after a higher than expected earnings report. However, the price slowly faded into the gap area after a couple of days. This fading into the gap area provides a great low-risk entry point for a trader. This point is considered low risk basically because you are able to measure the ease of selling compared to buying pressure. This means you can critically examine the supply and demand forces at a crucial point on the chart. The gap, in all these situations, provides a strong anchor point that can help support your position at these price levels. For instance, if you are a day trader and wish to buy the stock for trading purposes only, then you can use the gap to locate your stop loss indicators. For longer-term trades, you can place your stop loss measures on the other side of the gap. Basically, all companies that report good earnings were rewarded with steep share price increase before shares fall back to the post-earning gap area before finally rising from there. This strategy has been observed time and time again and is bound to work all the time.

Example: Consider CREE, the ticker symbol for Cree, Inc. This firm reported better than expected earnings that blew the lid through the roof. The profits went up by 100%. On the day of the announcement, the stock went up from $27.41 pre-announcement to $31.65. Then shortly thereafter, the excitement died down and the share eventually went down to $28.83. This still indicates a gain of 5% from the initial price. As a trader, you should wait for this frenzy to die down before eventually buying again.

Traders who waited for the drop are wise and definitely benefited from the gap. As a trader, you really want to buy low and sell high to make a profit. The share will continue to rise as the phenomenon and norm. The reverse is also true when shares underperform. This knowledge is crucial and can change the fortunes of an investor. It is the best strategy of

47

trading the post-earnings-announcement drift.

You can even earn more than 10% during a PEAD. The solution is to go for options. A good options trade can earn you a great profit. For instance, a 3% movement can translate to a 30% move in an option pairing and probably even more. Therefore, a less simple strategy such as options could enable you to maximize your profits.

As a trader, you should look for option pairs with an expiry date that does not exceed one or two months. Ensure that the share price is about a couple of dollars away from the current price. This is important because, in options trading, a small move in share price can mean a huge price in the options price. And with options, the closer they get to expiration, the more their value drops. So avoid acquiring options that are due to expire within the same month.

Chapter 6: Short Squeeze Setups: How High Short Interest Might Lead to Explosive Short-Term Moves

What is a Short Squeeze? It can be described as a situation where there is a lack of supply or demand in a particular stock. This causes a squeeze where the price of the security or stock rises sharply.

A short squeeze situation can occur within any trading time frame without preference. Even then, some of the most significant short squeezes tend to occur after a stock has gone through a continuous downward trend. As the security continues with its downward progression, day traders pounce on the dead cat bounces and increase their short squeeze opportunities.

As the number of traders seeking short positions continues to go up, an imbalance develops regarding the supply and demand of the stock. Soon thereafter, there will be an almost complete lack of the stock as traders buy all the stock. This short then leads to what is known as a squeeze.

Short Interest: The term "short interest" refers to the total stock or shares of a particular stock that have been sold short by buyers. This term is a measure of open short sales that have not yet been closed out or covered.

Short interest days to cover: This phrase refers to the number of shares that are shorted divided by the mean daily volume. Most new traders and investors wrongly believe that this term refers to the time that short sellers have to cover their short positions. This is absolutely inaccurate.

The terms to cover simply refers to a method of evaluating the chances of a short squeeze in a stock. This is done by measuring the future purchase pressure on a share that is likely to occur should the short sellers purchase back shares to close out their short positions.

What is short interest ratio? The term "short interest ratio" is simply another term for short interest days to cover ratio. To calculate this ratio, simply divide the total number of shares traded short by the daily trading volume.

This ratio points to the days it requires short sellers to repurchase any borrowed shares they owned. The ratio provides a sure method of measuring the probability of a short squeeze happening. Short interest days to cover that read above 3 indicate a clear short squeeze candidate. Also, as long as a company does not go bankrupt, then the chances of a short squeeze increase in relation to the number of days to cover reading.

Can you Profit from a Short Squeeze?

You need some skills and plenty of luck to benefit from. Most traders often check the days to cover and confirm through platforms such as NASDAQ on a bi-weekly basis. The traders will then discover if the ration of short shares to demand is high and so they will buy. However, most shares are unavailable on the markets often due to underperformance.

Traders would benefit more if they waited for the stock to approach what is known as a climatic volume event or even a multi-year support level. Such events will generate the necessary short-term purchase power that is essential. As a trader, you need to identify a good candidate for a short squeeze and then execute a great game plan that will see you emerge a winner having made huge profits.

It may not be easy for everyone to understand how a high short-interest can result in a large squeeze. This is because most stocks featuring high short-interest are often from poorly performing companies headed towards bankruptcy. However, such facts are of little interest to day traders or short-term traders.

On a short squeeze, many traders will try to exploit the supply and demand deficit with many believing there is free money to be made. Sadly, a lot of them are likely to lose money. High short interest translates to plenty of shares that need to be purchased in the open market. The end result will be plenty of eager buyers in the open market and limited supply which will prompt a price increase and buyers paying whatever price the sellers ask for.

Short Interest Reporting

Every listed company is required to provide short interest reporting. Such information should be submitted bi-weekly at all securities markets including NASDAQ, OTC, NYSE and all others. Short interest reporting is necessary so that investors, traders, and shareholders are made aware of any gross short interests that exist.

What causes a short squeeze? This situation occurs when there are excessive demand and a lack of supply of a given commodity. Most of the time, a short squeeze occurs when a stock's price rises to a level where short sellers need to make margin calls or count their losses and exit their positions. Short sellers trying to cover their positions will often buy shares which causes the price of the stock to rise even higher. In general, short squeeze situations often occur within stocks that have small floats and with a relatively small market capitalization.

The short squeeze does not return its gains all the time but it always showcases huge retracements once the squeeze comes to an end. Short squeezes often form what is known as V pattern peaks on charts. These are indicators that the purchasing that drives the stock upwards is not a real bullish purchase. It is more often a result of side demand that emanates from new orders or earnings surprises and so on. As soon as the short squeeze comes to an end, the stock often crashes down. Essentially, your success in trading the short squeeze will depend on your capacity to dispose of your stock towards the momentum when it is as close to the peak as possible. Any stocks that short the markets are often referred to as Bear ETFs where ETF means exchange-traded funds.

As a trader, you can easily trade in and out of any short ETF the same way you would trade a stock. There is no requirement to have a margin account as you are mostly going long on the short ETF in exactly the same way you would a stock.

Chapter 7: Huge Volume Setups: How to Quickly Grow a Small Account

Volume Setups:

Volume is simply a measure of the quantity of stock or other instrument that is traded at the markets within a given period of time. It refers to the number of shares that get to exchange hands over a certain time.

Volume is a crucial metric as it allows traders to find out the liquidity levels of a particular asset and, how easy or challenging it is to enter and exit a position as close to the prevailing price as possible.

Buying and Selling Volume

All traders know that the higher the volume of shares available the easier it is to purchase or sell large quantities of the shares because there are traders readily available to buy them. For a valid transaction to occur, there needs to be a willing seller and a willing buyer.

When trading shares, buyers are said to be in control when the price is pushed higher. On the other hand, sellers are said to be in control of a trade when the price is pushed lower. Volume is always displayed at the bottom of any stock price chart. It is normally indicated in vertical bars

On a daily chart, volume bars indicate the number of shares that exchanged hand in the course of a specific day. The bars are often colored. The red volume bar indicated a decline in price so the volume is considered a selling volume. On the other hand, the volume bar is green in color if the price goes up and the volume is then considered buying volume.

Relative Volume

A lot of traders prefer day trading stocks with huge volumes. This is because large volumes allow them to get in and out of trades fairly quickly. The term average volume refers to the number of shares of a particular stock that were traded on a regular trading day. Some days have large volumes while others see small volumes.

You need to focus your attention on days with higher than usual volumes because such days are often associated with large price movements and volatility. When most of the volume is seen at the bid price then the share price is likely to move lower while increased volume indicates sellers willing to exit from the trade.

Volume can Analyze Stock Price Movements

When you monitor volume, you can acquire useful statistics which can assist you in analyzing a stock's price movement. There are some guidelines or rules that you will need to follow. Here they are;

- Increased trade volumes simply indicate that traders and investors are pushing the price in either direction. If the price is moving upwards with increased volume then this shows that buyers are very eager to acquire the specific stock. Such moves are typically associated with huge upwards volume moves.

- It is possible for trends to persist even when volumes are in decline. But mostly, volumes tend to decline as the price does so indicate a weakening trend. For instance, should the trend be up with declining volumes, then this will indicate that there are fewer investors intending to purchase the stock to keep the price high. However, the trend will not necessarily change until there is more large-scale volume selling than buying.

- Volume should generally be bigger as the price moves towards the trending direction. It is lower when it moves against the trend. This is a great indicator or pointer that volume increases in the direction of the trend and decreases in the opposite direction of the trend. The trend could be weakening when there are high volumes accompanies by distinct yet sharp price movements against it.

Trading Volume

Volume is a very important aspect of your trades, especially as a day trader. You can use volume effectively to isolate the stocks you wish to trade on a particular trading day. Day trade stocks need to have sufficient volume to make it easy for traders to enter and exit.

The ability to exit and enter trades easily is a great way of minimizing losses and also makes it easy to collect profits when exiting. Volume is also useful in the analysis of a stock's trend at the market because it makes it easy to assess the likely hood that a trend will reverse or continue.

Guidelines for Using Volume to Grow an Account

For every buyer, there has to be a seller. Both are often in an ongoing battle for the best price in different time frames and this creates price movement. When analyzing volume, there are certain important guidelines that can be used to determine the strong and weak points of a move. Traders are generally inclined to avoid moves that portray a weakness and join moves that appear strong and beneficial.

Rising markets often result in rising trade volumes. Buyers need increased enthusiasm and increasing numbers to continue pushing prices upwards. Higher prices and lower volumes are pointers to a lack of interest in the market and this could lead to a reversal of the trend. In general, a price drop or even rise is a clear indicator that something has fundamentally changed.

Exhaustion Moves

Exhaustion moves are clearly visible in rising and falling markets. Exhaustion moves are simply sharp movements in the price of a share and they often signal the end of a particular trend. At the bottom of the market, falling prices cause lots of traders to quit resulting in increased volumes and volatility.

Watch out for bullish signs: Volume provides you with clear signs about bullish trends. For instance, if the price goes down and volume increases, then the price increases further while volume decreases, then it is okay to interpret this as a bullish sign.

Rising prices should ideally be followed by rising volume. When volumes are increasing and closes are within the upper portion of any range then the values will be quite high. But when the closes are in the lower portion then the values will go down. This is sometimes referred to as Chaikin money flow indicator.

It is clear to see that volume is a very important financial tool. There are many different ways of using it. Volume can be used to assess market weaknesses and strengths and to also confirm whether there is a reversal or even a price move. Indicators are very useful when making market decisions but volume on its own is not a very precise exit or entry tool. It should be used in conjunction with other indicators to provide firm information. For instance, looking at price action and a volume indicator will provide more accurate information.

Simple Volume Trading Strategies to Quickly Grow a Small Account

Volume is one of the oldest yet reliable day trading indicators. Volume analysis refers to a technique used to assess a trend in the stock market. In fact, volume is one of the most important indicators, especially for day traders. It is also among the simplest and most effective tools of observing the trading of a particular stock at the markets. Using volume, you can tell how many shares were bought and sold at a given trading period.

1. Volume and Breakouts: As a trader, you should always be on the lookout for points of support and resistance. Breakouts are always identified by two key indicators. These are volume and price. A breakout is considered suspect if it indicates a good price but without volume. In such a situation, a price reversal will most likely occur. As a day trader, you should wait until volume breaks the high of the day before you try and find an entry point.

When any stock that you are interested in starts breaking the high points, try and identify heavy volume. If you note any break with a high of 50% - 70% less volume, this is something else. Ideally, if you are trading within the margins then do not worry too much about a couple of a thousand shares. In an ideal situation, volume would expand at the breakout point which allows you to get most of the gains through the impulsive move higher.

Sometimes it is not possible to find out if a stock or share will have a breakout based on the information available. For instance, after observing a chart, you may be unable to tell if a stock will have definite breakout points. This is where financial management comes in handy as you now have to take your chances and actually enter a trade. You can tell if your trade will be successful by observing the volume. If it picks up on the breakdown, then you will know that the price action was successful.

2. Trending stocks and volume: As a stock keeps trending higher, you should look out for volume increase especially on each successive high and a decrease on successive lows. The real story here is that there is more positive volume when the stock starts to move higher as this confirms the health of the trend.

In such situations, the volume goes up in the same direction as the trend and this is something you are likely to observe throughout the day. With this strategy, you should wait for the trade to stabilize during the morning session then, take a look at developments after 11.00 in the morning. As your investment works in your favor, you should continue to observe the volumes and watch out for any chances of a trend reversal.

So with this strategy, always watch out for the volume that will push the stock towards the trend. Be ready to hold the stock for a couple of hours so that you really enjoy the rewards. As soon as you learn how to identify the relevant stocks that will trend all day, then you are good to go. Also, learn to use volume as an indicator to keep you winning and not to find a stock that will trend.

Growing a Small Trading Account

It is pretty challenging to grow a small trading account. It is estimated that over 90% of traders lose money and only 10% of them make any money. As a trader, you want to be among the 10% who are actually making money. Here are useful pointers that will enable you to grow a small account.

- *Always determine the risk versus reward ration before starting any trade activity.* If you enter a trade and the reward is $10 and the risk also worth $10, then do not enter such a trade. It is very important, as a trader, to enter trades where the reward far supersedes the risk. For instance, a good trade is one where the risk is $10 but the reward is $150 - $200. This way, you will lose $10 some of the time but make $200 at other times. Small losses are okay so you should keep this in mind as a trader. However, cut your losses quickly and find other trades that are profitable.

- *Ensure that you do not overtrade.* Most of the time, traders especially new ones, overtrade. This can be mentally exhausting and is a huge mistake. Traders who are doing well often want to trade more and make money all the time. No need to trade and lose, ending the day in the red. It is much better to wait until all the setups and indicators are there before entering a trade.

- *You should not be afraid of pulling profits or locking them in.* As a trader, you should feel okay to sell your stock and lock in the profits. Oftentimes, traders get greedy and let their stocks run a little longer. Remember, experienced traders say that you can never go broke taking profits. Also, use stop losses and all other important indicators but do not be afraid of taking profits. Trading can be lots of fun if done correctly. You should start out conservatively and enter only trades you are sure of winning.

Chapter 8: Bearish Setups:

How to make money during corrections

Bearish traders: A bearish trader is one who believes that a stock price will decline. As a trader, you can easily spot bearish trade setups if you carefully observe the markets.

When a stock is on an upward trend, it could experience short-term changes in direction to trend downwards. Once the short-term trend is over, the upward trend will resume. At the start of this new upward trend is what is referred to as a bearish setup which continues till the next peak, before another short-term decline.

Any good trader will wait for the correction to be completed so as to catch it at its peak. Your aim here is to anticipate the profit potential on the buy side as profits move upwards. You will also be looking to purchase the pullback position as well within the direction of the bigger upward trend. Always keep in mind that 3-wave moves are corrections while 5-wave moves tend to define the trend at large. Ideally, you want to determine the direction of the trade and then trade in the direction of the trend. Any time that the trend pauses for a correction provides a great opportunity to join. This will be the entry point.

The downward trends clearly indicate the bearish setups that we want to trade. Anytime a 5-wave move comes to an end, it will be retraced in three waves as a correction. The end of this wave signifies the best trading opportunity for this setup. You can take advantage of this setup as soon as the downward trend starts.

The classic wave pattern

The classic wave pattern contains 3-wave downs and 5-wave upwards. Such wave patterns provide you, the trader, with 4 different entry points. At any one of these 4 points, you can join the trend with high chances of profitable trades. You will be positioning yourself for towards the trend and then identify the exit or termination points of the trend.

What is a Correction?

A correction can be defined as a reversal of a stock movement, often negative, of about 10% or more. This usually occurs as the stock tries to adjust the price after an over-evaluation. Corrections can also be said to be temporary price declines that interrupt an upward trend of an asset or the entire market.

While a lot of traders may be uncomfortable with corrections, they are actually healthy and necessary for the markets. Traders and investors may not be happy to observe losses of 10% or more on shares that they hold, but these are most of the time good for the market. Stocks and commodities at the market are often volatile in the short-term but often exhibit strong tendencies in the long term. Stock markets have showcased a strong track record of success over many years. This is why there is a huge opportunity for traders and investors to make money during market corrections.

How to Profit from a Market Correction

Every now and then, the market goes through a correction. There are a couple of strategies for investing money during a correction. However, betting on market timing is rather difficult and some say even impossible. In reality, the markets can be as irrational as they want for much longer that a trader can remain solvent. Therefore, instead of engaging in a game that is impossible to win, it is best to adapt a strategy that you can win.

First Approach

As a trader, it is very important that you be prepared for the correction. What you can do is, assess the market and then come up with a list of stocks you'd love to own. So, have a watch list in the meantime. It is easier to do this online by creating a portfolio which can allow you to set up at some of the major finance platforms. Now you will need to regularly click on your portfolio of stocks and see how each is performing. Once the correction gets underway, you will be reminded of your stocks and then check to see how far they will fall.

Also, you can have it in such a way that the system provides you with even more details.

For instance, you can enter a price you think is the true worth of the stock and not the current value. For instance, if CitiGroup stock seems worth $30, then put a share of it in your portfolio and include that price. This way, you will be able to know how over or undervalued it is. You may probably have to revisit and correct the price occasionally.

Smart way to Benefit from Market Correction

Another approach you can use to benefit from a correction is to identify all the stocks trading at a discount price. This is especially true if the correction results from one particular sector. For instance, the falling price of oil has greatly affected the energy sector. Alternatively, take the financial services as another example. The sector performed poorly in recent times and stock prices might fall leading to a market correction. Therefore, you can take a closer look at the stock of some of the major banks and watch them for a while.

One of the smartest and best ways of profiting from the markets during a fall or correction is basically to imitate the action of major stock market investors such as Warren Buffett. This is easy to accomplish because the securities exchange commission of the US, the SEC, requires quarterly reports of the moves of major financial services players. You can get a hold of some of the transcripts which are publicly available and follow their investment pattern.

Yet another Method of Benefiting from Market Correction

Another great example of profiting from a market correction also happens to be one of the easiest and simplest to apply. This is a technique known as dollar cost averaging. The term "dollar cost averaging" may sound technical or even complex but it really refers to investing additional money in the same stocks. This is not just a simple investment technique but also enables you to invest in your portfolio for the long term and also enables you to benefit from each and every market correction. This is so because you will continue investing in your stocks even when the price hits rock bottom.

For instance, let us assume you invested about $300 in BAN or Bank of America ETF each month. Now for two years, you would have put in $7,200 into the ETF and probably also purchased about 200 shares each month at the share price prevalent each end month. You also re-invested the income back into your investment. Dollar costing average is a great way of making money during or immediately after a market correction. Some people assume that there are better ways of investing the money rather than buying at the market peak. However, not even the most seasoned investors and traders can get the timing right all of the time.

Step 4 of How to Benefit from Stock Market Correction

It is a documented fact that many traders and even investors just won't bother undertaking an in-depth analysis of a particular stock. Not even of ones that they are interested in buying. This is now unnecessary if you choose to invest or buy EFTs or exchange-traded funds that specifically target particular sectors of the market. If you are interested in a particular sector of the economy, such as finance, energy, manufacturing, and so on, then you can invest in EFTs and save yourself from the trouble of having to conduct in-depth, thorough research into some of these shares.

Simply follow your beliefs or passion about your preferred sector then put your money in your preferred EFT. It is possible that you will not necessarily get the best possible return by investing in ETFs as you will be exposed to many companies within your chosen sector. However, if your gut feeling or thesis, is correct and the stock in your chosen sector bounces back, then the ETF will definitely reflect these gains and you will have made some great returns on the back of a correction. Also, your investment will perform much better than if you had singled out a stock and invested solely in that particular stock.

Step Five of How to Benefit from a Market Correction

You can also focus on your chosen sector of the economy and invest in ETFs in that sector as well as purchase some stocks in one or more companies. Let us assume that you think the energy sector will recover soon but are unsure which specific shares will perform well. At this juncture, you would do well to first invest in an energy-related ETF as you continue with the analysis of the individual stocks in the sector. Once you are more informed about which stocks will rise in the energy sector after a thorough analysis, you can then proceed to sell your ETFs for a profit and then invest the money in specific energy stocks. This will ensure that you reap handsomely during a correction and benefit from both ETFs and stocks.

Bearish Setups and Corrections

Many traders prefer stock buyouts to make money when the market is in a downturn. As interest rates are way down during this period, well-resourced companies have very few ways of making an attractive return on their investment. It then becomes quite popular to buy the stock of undervalued companies. You can do your research and search for companies on the stock market.

Take for instance the firm Real Networks who ticker symbol is RNWK. This is considered by traders as a great stock to invest in especially during a correction. The reason is that its risk to reward ration goes up rapidly as its value drops. Even if all goes wrong, investors or traders would lose about $.45 per share. So the risk to reward ration in this instance is now about 12 to 1 which is pretty good. By investing in such shares and looking at their performance in the course of the correction, then traders could easily make a near profit.

Chapter 9:
Relative Strength Setups:

How to Gain from the Moves of Big Players

What is relative strength? The Relative Strength Indicator is a technical indicator that measures the strength or momentum of any gains and losses made by stock based on the closing price. These are often shown or indicated on candlestick charts over a given period of time. This helps traders to determine whether the stock has been oversold or overbought.

There is a simple formula for calculating the relative strength index. Relative strength is obtained by dividing the average gain with the average loss. The RSI or relative strength index calculation is determined based on 14 periods of time. There are important factors about this popular index. Here they are.

- The relative strength index is quite popular with traders and they use it to make an analysis on different markets such as the stocks, commodities, and money markets.

- The index is ideally a momentum oscillator which measures the size and direction of price movement relating to specific stocks.
- Momentum of stocks as the RSI index is calculated as the ratio of higher closes to lower closes. This basically means that should there be more candlesticks that close with higher gains, then the RSI will increase in value. But if there are candlesticks with lower gains, then the RSI will decrease in value.
- The RSI lies on a scale from 1 to 100. Traders commonly prefer to use two distinct levels. These are the 30 and 70 levels.

Information Revealed by the RSI Index

- When the RSI index is below 30, it simply means that the price is weak and has been on a downward trend.
- If the index is below the 30 value and is in the oversold area, this might mean the price is close to reversal.

- However, when the index is above the 70 level mark, then it is a strong indicator that the price has been performing quite well and is really strong.
- But if the RSI index is above 70 and in the area indicating a share has been over purchased, then the price may be due for a reversal.

Simple Ways of Trading the RSI Indicator

There are about 3 basic ways of trading stocks using the relative strength indicator. These are listed below.

1. Trade stocks when the index is in the oversold area. This means to buy more stock.
2. Trade the markets if the RSI index is within the overbought region. This translates to selling your stock.
3. Trade anytime you notice a divergence of the index. This basically implies that the RSI index and the share price are trending in opposing directions. As such, you are likely to notice the price going for higher highs yet on the

indicator window the RSI will be on a lower high. This kind of behavior is also known as a divergence.

Trading an RSI in the Oversold Region

This is a pretty straightforward technique. What you need to do is confirm that the market is on a downward trend. Now check whether the RSI index has crossed below the 30-mark level because this is a good indicator that it is not in the oversold region so there is a high probability the price will start to head back up.

So for now, simply wait for the RSI line to head towards the 30 level region and then past it. Once the 30-mark level is surpassed, then you can proceed to purchase the relevant stock.

Trading an RSI Index in the Overbought Region

This approach is the exact opposite of the previous one. Here, we first confirm that the market is already on an upward trend. Now check to see that the RSI index has already crossed over and above the 70-mark level.

This will be a clear indicator the stock has entered the overbought region with potential for the price to begin a downward trend. Once this becomes obvious, simply sit back and wait for the RSI to begin its downturn at least until it touches the 70-mark level. Once this level is surpassed, then you are free to sell the stock.

Selling or Trading on an RSI Index Divergence

If you are to successfully and profitably sell on the RSI divergence, then you need to be able to notice the sell trading setup then purchase the trading setup once it begins to form. First, ensure that the RSI oscillator line is clearly and well over the 70-mark level. This is a necessary condition if you are to trade the RSI divergence.

During an upward trend, the price of the stock should show a high that corresponds to a similar high by the RSI indicator. However, you are likely to observe the RSI index when the price gets to the next higher high. When this happens then you will receive the information that RSI divergence has occurred with the potential of a price increase so be ready to sell your stock.

Tips on How to Use the RSI Effectively

When there are sudden price movements in the stock market, false sell or buy signals can be generated on the index. Therefore, avoid using it on its own and instead use other indicators as well to confirm whether the signals are genuine or not.

There are traders who, instead of using additional markers, choose to apply quite extreme values of the RSI ratio. These are used as the sell or buy signals, for instance, readings above 80 or below 20. The figures above 80 are supposed to indicate an overbuy situation while the figure below 20 is meant to indicate an oversell situation.

This index is sometimes used together with trend lines because the trend line resistance and support often point to resistance and support levels of the RSI index. As a trader, you need to be on the lookout for convergence or divergence that occurs between the RSI indicator and the stock price. This is yet another reliable way of making use of the indicator.

Ideally, divergence takes place whenever a stock hits a new high or low in its price without the RSI index making a corresponding new low or high value. There are both bearish and bullish points of divergence.

A bearish divergence can be described as the situation where the price makes a new high while the RSI index does. This divergence is viewed as a sell signal. On the other hand, a bullish divergence occurs when the price of a stock hits a new but the RSI index does not do so. This is then considered as a purchase signal.

Take the example of a stock that sees an increase in price to $50. Now the RSI index goes to indicate a high reading of 65. Then the stock experiences a slight retraction in the downward direction. The stock then goes on to hit a new height of $55 while the RSI gets to only 60. This shows that the RSI has diverged and taken a bearish position and has generally diverged from the price movement.

The Downside of the Relative Strength Indicator

Every indicator has its benefits and downside. While the RSI index is a great indicator when trading the markets, there are chances that price tops and price bottoms can occur much later after the overbought and oversold zones are reached. This means that when an RSI is below the 30-mark level in the oversold region, there is no guarantee that once this happens the price will start going up.

Also, the indicator can stay in the overbought or oversold region for a much longer period of time especially in a strong trending market. This can give a false buy or sell signal. It is advisable, therefore, to use more indicators to confirm the necessary trades. You can use charts and other indicators mentioned above.

Learn and Benefit From Moves of the Big Players

Big investors may not agree on much but they do generally agree that generating big profits in the markets needs a relentless strategy and plan that revolves around a solid set of rules. A lot of beginners and small-time traders jump into the market with very little knowledge of the markets. Most of the time you sold too early, probably didn't understand what terms such as spread mean and so on.

Learn to Separate Substance from Fluff

As a trader, you need to be able to filter out market noise. This is an essential requirement if you are to succeed and make big money investing in the stock market. You also need to take the three important actions of investing. These are;

- Zeroing in on volume and price action
- Focus closely on a stock's fundamentals and chart activity
- Ignore just about everything else

Things you should Ignore

There are certain bits and pieces of information that you should not pay heed to. For instance, if a friend or relative reveals that a certain firm is about to receive a government contract, then you should ignore such information. It should be treated as a rumor and not factual information.

A columnist or commentator may claim that a potential investment is not worth your time simply because they have concerns that have no history on stock activity. Such thoughts are not well reasoned and should, therefore, be ignored. Even information from analysts that have not been properly analyzed should be treated like noise and ignored.

Instead, you should do what big investors often do. They study stocks and listen to the markets in silence. You can also study the actions of big investors and observe what it is that they do. For instance, search and find out which fund owned what stock and whether a particular trend in ownership tends downwards or upwards.

Watch Fund Managers

Lots of the time, market analysts and columnists are often ignored even when they offer their opinions on TV and elsewhere. Basically, fund managers are the experts to watch because their actions determine the outcome of trades at the markets. For instance, they will never talk bad about a stock but will sell it. Also, they never unnecessarily praise a stock but instead, they invest in it. Therefore, watch their actions and learn from what they do.

Watch Major Stocks

You should also watch the activity of major stocks and shares. You can find this information readily available on different websites and platforms. Sometimes the information shows which funds hold which stocks and in what quantity. This kind of information is very important and helps to ensure that you are in the know about what stocks can move the markets in a big way.

Have your Own Set of Investing Rules

As a trader, you should craft your own rules that will guide you as you trade and invest in the stock market. You can start by asking successful investors what type of rules they followed, what their investment policies or principles that they followed to be so successful. Here are some policies that will guide you when you are looking to buy and invest in stocks.

1. Be patient with winning trades and impatient with losing trades.

This is a great rule to live by, declared by Dennis Gartman, who often advises hedge fund managers, mutual funds, trading firms, and brokerage firms. He is also an accomplished trader and regular commenter on finance networks. According to Mr. Gartman, it is very possible to make plenty of money if you are correct 30% of the time so long as profits are large and losses small.

This rule also advises on a couple of other mistakes that traders often make. For instance, a trader is likely to sell at the first sign of profit. Instead, Gartman advises to let a winning trade continue its run. Also, traders should not allow a losing trade to get away. Investors are generally okay with losing a little bit of money but not a lot of it. Remember, therefore, that you do not have to be right most of the time. Remember too, that it is okay to lose a little bit of money but not a lot.

2. It is better to buy into a wonderful company at a fair price than buy a fair company at a wonderful price.

This is a great rule followed by Warren Buffett. Warren is considered as the most successful stock market investor in history. He is one of the richest men in the world and has advised numerous US presidents. And whenever Warren talks, the markets listen. His letters and teachings to his investment firm are used by top business schools to teach finance students.

Buffett offers two crucial pieces of advice. One is, when investing in a company, always look at its fundamentals. This means listening to conference calls, observing the balance sheets and having confidence in the firm's management. The second piece of advice is to only look at the price and evaluate it once the quality of the company has been affirmed. Traders should not expect to buy shares of a quality company at throwaway prices but at fair, market value prices. Also, do not buy the shares of a poorly performing company even if they are priced really low.

3. If you really like a stock, then put at least 10% of your money into it

This is advice that's been put forward by Bill Gross. Bill is one of the founders of PIMCO which is the among the world's biggest bond funds on the globe. His statement above speaks mostly about investment rather than trading. According to Bill, you really should diversify your portfolio and never put all your money in one box.

As an investor, you also have to take chances in the market based on well-informed research. Also, always have some cash in your accounts to fund those trades that may require a little more capital.

Chapter 10: Mean Reversion Setups: When is the Right Time to go Against a Trend?

What is mean reversion trading?

The term "mean reversion trading" is also known as the counter-trend or simply reversal trading. In this kind of trade, you will be looking for stock prices that have shifted significantly away from the mean price. Essentially, the mean reversion strategy seeks unsustainable trends.

To calculate the mean price of a commodity or stock, use the moving average and then apply it to the charts. If you observe the charts closely, you will notice that the price attempts a reversion to numerous times but failed. This means that the mean reversion strategy is more than just a trading towards the moving average. This kind of trade requires risk management approach, a very strict entry management and an emotionally stable investor who will not over trade or seek revenge trading.

Overcome Challenges and Trade Successfully

There are a couple of challenges that traders often encounter during mean reversion trading. Here are some important aspects to consider.

How to determine the mean: Finding out the mean sounds pretty easy but plenty of times, traders never focus on the implications of the choice of moving average and how it affects their trade. You can apply two different moving averages such as the 50 smoothed moving average and the 100 smoothed moving average. While the difference may seem unimportant, identifying the correct one is absolutely essential for a successful trade. There are significant differences between the moving averages so ensure that the correct one is chosen.

Price may not reverse: In some cases, the price does not reverse. This is an overlooked aspect and sometimes undervalued. It happens because the reversal occurs very slowly while the moving average inches closer to the price. This tends to reduce the reward obtained from the trade. You need to appreciate that sometimes the moving average inches up to the price at a faster rate and can undermine the final earnings of a trade. As a trader, you have to decide if you will move the take profit together with the moving average or leave initial take profit order unaltered.

Mean reversion or grabbing a falling knife: It is considered quite risky to pick tops and bottoms even though green traders often do this. It occurs because traders are at times unaware that price can trend for a lot longer. It is important that during periods of string trends that last a long while, it is possible to lose money – unless, of course, if precaution is taken. This kind of trading does not mean waiting at predetermined levels with pending orders. It is much better to wait just until the movement comes to a standstill and indicators point to the happenings in the market.

Discipline and emotional stability: While these tenets apply to all forms of trade, they are especially important when it comes to mean reversion trading. Sometimes it takes a very long while for trade signals or price movements to occur. As a trader, you may feel that you waited too long and your desired entry criteria may not yet be visible. It is very important at this stage that you do not jump in too late or sometimes even too early trying to chase a trade. Even after everything else works out in your favor the price might still work against you so always be on the lookout. Do not cut your losses just yet simply because you believe that the reversal is due.

All these important points indicate the complexity and challenges of trading a mean reversion. The complexity becomes obvious why this particular trade is not absolutely suitable for everyone. Traders struggling with the mental aspect of trading and, those who are new to complex strategies may wish to add to their knowledge and experience first before embarking on this kind of trade.

Trading Against the Trend

As a trader, it is advisable to trade with the trend always. This is a long-standing adage that always works. The trend is supposed to be your friend even as you trade, no matter what.

Determine the direction of the trend

The first thing you need to do is to determine the direction of the market. This is where the rule, KISS (keep it short and simple) comes into play. To determine the trend's direction just follow a simple rule that will guide you. When considering the trend, remember to take time frames into consideration. For instance, if you want to consider a long-term trade, you will need to use the long-term time frame.

In reality, longer time frames often dominate the shorter ones but for some purpose, the shorter ones are more useful and often prevail. In short, they provide more value. Take the case of a major company investing in a foreign company. Such a company could be more interested in the long-term outlook of the country's currency while speculators may only be interested in short-term outlook.

Tools for Determining Long-term Trends

We can use a weekly chart to determine the long-term trends of a speculative trade. You will need two simple tools -- the exponential moving average as well as the simple moving average or SMA. Consider a random chart from 2006. Let us assume the chart indicates that between May and July of the same year, the blue 20 interval period exponential moving average was above the red 55 simple moving average. However, both were on the upward momentum and sloping upwards. This actually shows that the trend is rising.

Sometimes, trends tend to change. For instance, using the above example, the trend started to head downwards for both the averages. When the simple moving average and the exponential moving average move downwards, then the trend is heading downwards. You can use the same moving averages. The aim is to determine the trend and not the exit or entry points. When you want to trade with the trend, then you need to wait for the correction. Therefore, you can choose to either trade against the trend or simply wait until the trend heads in the upward direction to trade.

Strategies to Invest Against the Trend

There are plenty of investors who put their money in the market and leave it there for many years. They assume that since it is in the markets, it will grow and yield high profits over time. This kind of thinking is misguided in some instance. The buy-and-hold strategy may work but there are better approaches for long-term investment.

There are many things that could happen and your earnings in a buy-and-hold account wiped out. To be safe, you may want to consider investing against the market. You can choose from a couple of strategies that are regularly used. These, if well implemented, could see you reap huge benefits in a relatively short period of time.

Trade Using Options

You can trade the markets using options. Options trading pairs two related stocks and provides lots of opportunities to traders. For instance, traders are set to benefit from leverage, liquidity, and versatility. You also get a chance to bet against a stock and essentially against the trend.

Options trading is more often a very complex way of trading and is not the best alternative for newbies and inexperienced traders. Basically, options trading gives you a chance to buy an options contract where you can buy or sell a stock at a specified price on a given date. Simply put, when you buy an options contract, you can easily trade against the trend.

Trade Using the Shorting Technique

You can also trade against the trend through a process known as shorting. Plenty of traders have probably never even heard about the term "Shorting a stock." Even those who have heard about it have probably not put it into practice just yet. Any time you short a stock, you actually do not yet own the stock as at that very moment. What you do is agree to sell the stock to a buyer because you hope to purchase the same stock from another trader or investor at a much lower price and at a later date. For instance, a person shorting a stock would offer to sell a $50 stock at probably $55 to an interested buyer. In the meantime, the seller will be waiting for the price to go down to buy the stock cheaply.

It is important to be very careful when executing this shorting process. This is because you agree with a buyer to sell them shares or stocks that you do not own or have. These kinds of transactions have only marginal profits yet could cost you huge sums of money should things go wrong. If the price of the stock was to go up before maturity of your agreement, then you would most likely lose money. However, if, after your analysis, you are certain that the price will go up, then this method has the capacity to be very lucrative as well.

Trade Inverse ETFs

If you do not want to trade in either shorting or options, another alternative you have is trading inverse ETFs. This is a better alternative and allows you to confidently bet against the market, but without any of the complex issues that affect options or shortening. The only challenge with this stock is that it does not let you bet against a particular stock but rather on the market in general.

Trading against the Trend

There are a number of instances when you may have to trade against a trend. There are reasons why markets fluctuate so much. When traders enter and exit a trade a dozen or more times, this tends to result in price fluctuations. At some point in their learning cures, traders get a chance to pause and observe the markets, eventually getting a chance to make more objective decisions. One of the concepts such traders use is trading with the trend.

There are traders who can, at some point, afford to go against the trend and still make money. There are different kinds of traders out there. They include scalpers, swing traders, and day traders. Scalpers are the traders that can afford to wage war against the trend since they often seek small profits. As a swing trader, you can take a counter trend for a small time frame.

For instance, let us assume there is a bullish trend on the market. The price appears to be pulling back on a 15-minute chart. On this chart, the trend appears to be bearish in the shorter time frame. You can at this point get into the trade and go against the trend. This is because the larger view indicates a bullish trend even though the smaller time chart indicates a bearish trend. What you will be looking for as you enter the trend is for stability on the 15-minute chart then find an entry point.

The interest here is actually in the long outlook. You will likely emerge the winner should the hourly bullish trend continue even though the short term is bearish. However, even as you trade, you need to assess your risks and ensure that everything aligns itself according to your plan. It if all makes sense in the end, then you should be able to make a neat profit even though in the short run only.

Always remember that, as a professional trader, you need to be able to adapt to different situations. Do not label or box yourself in any one type of trading but actually accept to be flexible. By combining both aspects of trade, you stand a better chance of success as a trader. There are plenty of people who consider trading against the trend as dangerous and a venture that is too risky. Many traders have successfully tried to trade both sides of the trend. This approach favors some and might not favor others. However, for beginners, novices and newbies, it's safer getting experience first.

Conclusion

Thank you for making it through to the end of this book, let's hope it was informative and it provided you with all of the tools you need to achieve your goals whatever they may be.

The next step is to refine your trading skills and see which techniques in this book can make you a much better trader. While theories are great, it is all vanity unless it is put to good use. Try and apply the techniques taught here and see how well you will fare. You just might discover a better way to trade.

Finally, if you found this book useful in any way, a review on Amazon is always appreciated!